WHAT DEGREE DO I NEED TO PURSUE A CAREER IN INFORMATION TECHNOLOGY & INFORMATION SYSTEMS?

DAVID KASSNOFF

ROSEN
PUBLISHING®

Published in 2015 by The Rosen Publishing Group, Inc.
29 East 21st Street, New York, NY 10010

Copyright © 2015 by The Rosen Publishing Group, Inc.

First Edition

Library of Congress Cataloging-in-Publication Data

Kassnoff, David, author.
What degree do I need to pursue a career in information technology and
information systems?/David Kassnoff.—First edition.
     pages cm.—(The right degree for me)
Audience: Grades 7–12.
Includes bibliographical references and index.
ISBN 978-1-4777-7865-4 (library bound)
1. Computer science—Vocational guidance—Juvenile literature.
2. Information technology—Vocational guidance—Juvenile literature.
I. Title.
QA76.25.K37 2015
004.023—dc23

                                                    2014010972

Manufactured in the United States of America

CONTENTS

INTRODUCTION

Today, thousands of people download new music, apply for jobs, or use a debit card to buy lunch. Each of these transactions involves the sharing of digital information. Many of the world's business, entertainment, energy, education, health care, government, and military systems rely on being able to quickly and effectively manage, share, and safeguard electronic or digital information. On the home front, when there's a power outage in a community or someone's tablet can't connect to a network, it's often the result of an unexpected disruption in digital information.

Because so many everyday communications and transactions are performed digitally these days, it should come as no surprise that information technology and information systems—fields that dwell in the digital world—are among the fastest-growing careers today. The information technology (IT) and information systems fields encompass a range of career opportunities. These include software development, programming, and systems analysis, as well as jobs that emphasize research and inventing new technologies.

When someone refers to "information technology," many people imagine large corporations

Large organizations rely on
network engineers to help
design, maintain, and upgrade
network servers. These servers
process hundreds of thousands
of data requests each day.

that create software, data management systems, and computer hardware. Names such as
Adobe, Apple, Microsoft, Oracle, SAP, Hewlett
Packard, and Google, which are some of the
largest global IT businesses, spring to mind. But
IT is a thriving occupation in local businesses
and services as well. Hospitals and health insurance companies have large IT staffs. Supermar-
ket chains and mass retailers rely on complex

computer networks to monitor inventories and pur-
chasing patterns. The websites of most businesses
feature career pages that are full of job openings for
computer systems analysts, database administrators,
and network technical specialists. Public school systems also run on computers that monitor student
attendance, academic performance, and other important record-keeping functions. Even small businesses
from family farms to veterinarians to local shops
depend on information technologies.

The popularity and necessity of digital technology
has created a demand for qualified individuals to work
in the IT and information systems fields, and the need
keeps growing. Titles for these jobs include database
administrator, systems analyst, and technical support
specialist. Some IT positions emphasize research and
inventing new technologies. Others modify or upgrade
software programs used in real-world business situa-
tions. Still others in the IT industry focus on managing
and protecting digital information. There is a veritable
rainbow of IT career opportunities, and, as in real life,
the colors of a rainbow sometimes blur from one hue
to the next. Some IT professionals perform tasks that
encompass several of these duties.

Sound like an attractive and promising career path?
Read on to find out more about these fields, as well
as what type of training and education could make
dreams of working in IT a reality.

CHAPTER ONE

Cracking the Code

L et's start with a look at what information technology and information systems are about, namely data manipulation, storage, and retrieval. Almost any electronic device used in the home or at school has some set of preprogrammed commands or built-in code that helps it perform its tasks. In a smartphone or digital music player, it's called firmware. In a computer or tablet, it's called an operating system. Computers and similar devices rely on code to ensure that commands are delivered and interpreted effectively. At its core, code is a complex string of instructions and commands called algorithms. To most people, these algorithms appear on a screen as

```
»    alert(· "<?php·echo·
}·<?php·}·?>
<?php·if(·$this->item->
$this->item->linkparts[
$this->item->linkparts[
else·if(·document.getEl
»    alert(·"<?php·echo·
}·<?php·}·?>
```

Almost every electronic device relies on coded commands to operate as designed. Learning to write code is a critical skill for IT professionals.

symbols and numbers. Code is invisible to users of everyday electronic devices. To a smartphone or tablet, however, it is communication that tells the device to play music, capture and upload a photo or video, or take part in an online game with friends.

IT professionals may not be expert coders, but they at least understand how code works to make computerized electronics operational.

Jobs in Information Technology

In the information technology field, people with different types of skills work on different areas of software, networks, and the devices that use them. Titles for these individuals include chief information officer, IT manager, database administrator, systems analyst, and information security analyst.

Chief Information Officer (CIO)

Also known as chief technology officer, the chief information officer is usually the top decision-maker regarding IT systems in an organization. He or she relies on other IT managers, analysts, and team members to create, test, install, and de-bug the organization's software and hardware. The CIO often brings past experience in the jobs described above and has experience in several areas of information systems, as well as a background in business management. He or she frequently reports to an organization's president or chief executive officer.

One benefit of the IT workplace is that many jobs allow you to dress casually, especially in start-up high-tech companies.

IT Manager

The more formal title for IT manager is computer and information systems manager. These individuals plan, organize, and lead an organization's computer-related activities. They work with other decision-makers in an organization to figure out the organization's IT needs, hire IT programmers to support those needs, and direct the activities necessary to meet the organization's information management goals.

Database Administrators

Database administrators oversee the storage and organization of information, or data, so it can be

Here, an IT technician uses code stored on a laptop computer to modify the code used by the larger network servers.

accessed and shared by many. An important role of a database administrator is working to make certain the digital information is secure from hackers and unauthorized users outside the network. To do this, database administrators work with information security analysts and systems analysts.

Systems Analysts

Computer systems analysts evaluate an organization's current computer systems and procedures to determine how they can operate more efficiently and better serve the organization's needs. They evaluate

BY THE NUMBERS

The U.S. Bureau of Labor Statistics has reported that the job outlook for computer systems analysts was expected to grow 22 percent between 2010 and 2020. For database administrators, careers were expected to grow 31 percent, compared to the national average for all occupations of just 14 percent. Put another way, candidates with degrees in information technology will continue to be in high demand through at least 2020, and likely beyond.

emerging technologies and new software applications from both a business and IT point of view. They analyze the costs, quality, and benefits of these upgrades and recommend whether the upgrades will help the organization become more effective.

Other IT Jobs

Information security analysts work to protect an organization's data from hackers and cyberattacks. Computer network architects create and refine the internal systems that link all employees' computing devices within an organization, even if they work in separate locations. Finally, there are the computer support specialists, who help people and businesses fix problems with software, hardware, and database connectivity.

CHAPTER TWO

Choosing to Compute

With the many opportunities in the information technology field, how does someone choose which path to take? What degrees will get you where you want to go? Educational opportunities abound, including two- or four-year degree programs at community colleges and universities. Students who choose to attend college may choose to major in IT disciplines. They may also pursue studies in business, health care, or engineering that enable them to specialize in a field that relies on information management—perhaps while taking IT courses as a minor.

Trying to choose a degree path for your IT career? You have plenty of company, as thousands of students explore careers in IT and information systems.

Another choice future IT workers have to make is whether to pursue an undergraduate degree or travel

A high school computer lab is where many students first learn computing concepts, including writing simple programs using BASIC (Beginner's All-Purpose Symbolic Instruction Code) or Visual BASIC language.

down the vocational path and earn certification in their chosen field. Certification programs are available through vocational or technical schools. Certification is a good choice for students who enjoy the practical, hands-on aspects of building and maintaining computer equipment and networks, rather than focusing on computer languages to create and test software and codes.

MATH MASTERY

Today's IT industry involves multiple programming languages, platforms, and networking decisions. It's hard to acquire the necessary skills for success in the field without a solid, broad-based academic foundation. An IT education starts as early as high school and focuses heavily on math.

While there are exceptions, an education in mathematics, including pre-calculus, helps prepare high school students to transition to IT courses. It's not impossible to succeed in information technology without a command of math, but a mastery of math throughout high school will prepare you for coursework involving calculus, computer programming languages (such as C++ or C#), statistics, and assembly language programming.

Certifiably IT

Certificate programs provide good, basic exposure to the technologies and theories involved in information technology. Many certificate programs are geared to applied or practical career pursuits. These programs often focus on the day-to-day use of computers and digital systems to manage data and produce materials for business. There is much less emphasis on developing software, websites, games, and applications because most job options for people with a certificate do not involve these tasks. Therefore, it is important to decide if getting into a hands-on technician's role quickly is important. If not, the certificate coursework can help students "launch" into additional studies toward an associate's or bachelor's degree.

For example, Victor Valley Community College (VVCC) in Victorville, California, awards a certificate of achievement (CA) for the completion of programs of eighteen

The data center is the heart of an organization's network architecture. Data centers consist of multiple networked servers and serve as an "electronic library" of the organization's digital information.

or more units (credits). CAs, which are approved by the California Community Colleges Chancellor's Office, are recorded on students' official college transcripts and are transferable toward an associate's degree program. VVCC also awards a certificate of career preparation (CP), which recognizes completion of a sequence of fewer than eighteen units, approved by the VVCC Board of Trustees. Students earn a paper award, but the certificate doesn't appear on the student's college transcript.

Victor Valley Community College offers one associate's degree and several certificates in computer information technology. These options emphasize practical training that would be valuable in the computer programming workplace:

- Associate in Science, Computer Information Systems
- Database Administration Certificate
- MySQL Database Developer Certificate
- NetWare Certificate
- Network Specialist Certificate
- Programming I Certificate
- Programming II Certificate
- Productivity Software Specialist Certificate
- UNIX Administrator Certificate
- Visual Basic Programming Certificate
- Web Authoring Certificate

Other certificate programs may be more general, structured more to help students get their "feet wet" in a particular academic area than to train them for a specific job. For example, if a student is uncertain

ANOTHER KIND OF IT CERTIFICATE

Princeton University's Center for Information Technology Policy offers undergraduate students a certificate in Technology and Society, Information Technology Track. This program provides students with an understanding of the technologies used in IT and their impact on economic development, health care, politics, education, productivity, government, and other aspects of society. There is no direct career path associated with this certificate, but it can be useful in many areas of study, such as public policy or health care administration.

whether an IT programmer track meets his or her long-term goals, a certificate program provides a path to explore this discipline, and the credits earned can sometimes be transferred to a program that suits the student's long-term needs.

Depending on the institution, some certificate programs are offered in distance or online learning formats. This option provides the chance to take courses online to help decide if the discipline is in line with a student's career pursuits. Among the broader certificate programs that tie in with information technology are:

- Electronics Technology—an intermediate step for students pursuing further studies in applied sciences (that can lead to an associate in advanced science, or AAS degree). Typical courses include electronics technologies, AC/DC circuit analysis, computer applications for technicians, and technical mathematics.

- Computer Technician—often offered as a two-course program, this step introduces the student to basic concepts and mechanics of PC support, with emphasis on the concepts at this basic level. A second step adds emphasis on the mechanics of computer technology.
- Mathematics—a certificate program that helps prepare students for mathematics programs in four-year colleges or universities. A four-year mathematics degree can be a useful springboard to a career in information technology.

Students should seriously consider whether or not a certificate program could help them get a job or advance their career. A certificate may help set you apart from applicants without a certification. Academically, completing a certificate program shows that a student is interested in the field as well as continuing his or her education. Successfully completing a certificate program prepares the student for more in-depth college studies.

Beyond these factors, a certificate program can help students decide if an IT career path is worth pursuing. If the certificate program is easy to complete, it could very well be a signal that a more challenging degree path should be the next goal.

CHAPTER THREE

IT in Two Years

Colleges offering two-year and four-year IT degrees provide many opportunities for students. Finding the right college requires some research, often at the nearest library.

To succeed in programming, administration, and IT security jobs, a richer course of study than a certification program is essential. IT is an industry that advances quickly, adopting new programming languages and applications every year or two. It is therefore critical that workers in this field have a solid foundation in programming languages and coding, which a college degree can provide. An overwhelming number of IT job listings state that the employer is looking for candidates with some type of degree. A two-year degree program, in which students earn an associate's degree, offers a more focused educational experience than a certificate alone.

The Two-Year Basics

IT associate's degree programs enable students to complete some of the fundamental requirements of most four-year bachelor's degree programs. Many community colleges and vocational schools offer two-year programs in information technology, and the credits earned are often transferable to a four-year university. Online and on-campus options are widely available. They often emphasize the practical and technical aspects of how IT is used in accounting, marketing, database management, technical writing, and network security. Courses focus on computer security, database construction, problem solving, project management, and programming.

Many of today's college lecture halls have state-of-the-art technology. On a college visit, try sitting in to listen to a professor's lecture and interaction with students.

At the community college level, an IT or computer science program contains a blend of theoretical courses and applied courses, plus general education and electives. These focus on the study of basic computing principles and specific applications in which information can be managed or manipulated to solve problems. In general, students can expect to spend about eighteen to twenty-four credits in each of three areas of study: the major itself, general education classes (English, math, study skills, etc.), and electives such as physical education, business, and foreign languages.

The Associate of Science Degree

The most typical two-year IT degree is the associate in science (A.S.) degree. These degrees enable students to transfer to universities offering four-year bachelor of science (B.S.), bachelor of technology (B.Tech), or bachelor of arts (B.A.) degrees. Colleges and universities offer several types of IT programs leading toward such a degree, including:

- "Pure" computing in such university departments as computer information systems and straight-on computer science (plenty of math and science required)
- Information technology, which prepares students for employment in database management, systems programming, and network engineering (emphasizing computer languages and applications)

PROGRAM EXAMPLE

Northern Virginia Community College (NOVA)—with campuses in Alexandria, Manassas, Annandale, and other Virginia towns—offers an information systems technology associate in applied science degree (A.A.S.). This two-year degree program prepares students for information technology employment and serves to update the skills of those already in the field. Within this program are several two-semester study tracks leading to certificates in application programming, database specialization, IT technical support, network administration, and network engineering. Thanks to this setup, students can earn two related certifications in different aspects of IT as part of a two-year program.

In addition to the associate in applied science IT degree, NOVA also offers a two-year associate of science degree in information technology. Unlike the A.A.S. degree that emphasizes job-related studies, NOVA's IT A.S. degree is designed for students who plan to transfer to a four-year college or university to complete a bachelor's degree program in information technology.

- Management information systems (MIS), which is taught within a business major

Advantages of the Two-Year Path

What are some of the reasons to choose an associate's degree program? Let's start with choosing a career direction. It's not easy! Many students struggle to determine if they're on a path that matches their skills and passions. Two-year programs can serve as a kind of a testing ground in this regard. Courses taken at a community college allow students to get a grasp of the material and career opportunities associated with the coursework, without committing to a four-year degree. Also, associate's degree programs can be a good way to discover whether the academic requirements of a particular IT program—many require a strong math background, for instance—are manageable for individual students. Community colleges and state universities frequently offer study support services that can help students figure out if they can handle the requirements.

Community colleges may have smaller class sizes than large public or private universities. Introductory classes at four-year universities sometimes have hundreds of students, while in community college, average class sizes range from twenty-five to forty-five students. Smaller class sizes make it easier to ask questions, talk to instructors and classmates, and understand the lessons and assignments.

Community colleges can offer more flexible scheduling than a four-year school. Many offer more sections of the same class at different times, making it easier to

The smaller class sizes for introductory courses at community colleges can make it easier to connect with professors.

schedule classes around work and other responsibilities. Community colleges offer classes during the day, later in the evening, and sometimes on weekends to accommodate students' work schedules and family commitments.

Cost Considerations

The best reasons for attending a community college have much to do with focusing on the basics of a student's college education—and doing it affordably. The cost of tuition at a community, technical, or junior college is less than that of a four-year college or university, so earning an associate's degree at one of these places can save money. How much? Tuition varies widely between a community college, a public university, and a private university. When all is said and done, however, attending a community college saves moderately over a four-year public university and substantially over a private four-year institution of higher learning.

With lower fees and cost per credit hour, students can complete the requirements of a two-year degree for less money than a four-year college. Credit for core courses—which are those that cover basic, general academic disciplines such as English composition, math, and so on—are largely transferrable to four-year colleges and universities. This means the core courses could be completed at a community college at a lower cost per course than at a public or private university. Students can save some green by completing core requirements at a community college and then concentrating on the requirement toward the IT major when transferring to a four-year college.

Additionally, most community colleges attract local, perhaps regional students to their classrooms—people who, as the name suggests, live in the college's "community." They are not designed for on-campus living, as many four-year colleges are. Students attending local community colleges while working toward associate degrees can save on room and board by living at home or in less expensive off-campus housing.

All in Good Time

It is important to remember that a two-year degree isn't simply a shortcut to a four-year degree. Students in community colleges work hard, whether they take their classes on campus or complete a portion of them online. Time management is just as important in a two-year degree program as it is when working toward a bachelor's degree, and the commitment to doing the work and satisfying the requirements is the same as well.

Also, students should keep in mind that a two-year degree may take longer than two academic calendar years. Those who are juggling a job, family commitments, and college courses may need to finish one or more remaining courses after two years of study. How quickly an associate's degree can be earned depends on how students manage their time and other responsibilities.

CHAPTER FOUR

Four-Year Degrees and Beyond

B ecause IT is a hot field, it is not hard to find a four-year college or university offering a strong academic program to develop an expertise in IT and information systems. The field is expanding so rapidly that many colleges also offer wide-ranging coursework that allows students to obtain a bachelor's and a master's degree in five years. Students can earn an information technology degree at a brick-and-mortar university or online, sometimes making use of both methods.

Coursework

As with vocational and two-year degree programs, IT degree programs at four-year colleges focus on the technical aspects of the profession and link those aspects to how businesses use technology. The IT-specific coursework varies a bit from school to school, but the basics cover courses such as an introduction to programming and programming languages, data management, network administration, systems analysis, and security issues.

Most four-year degree programs begin with an introductory or survey course. The emphasis is on computer design and functionality. This "101," or intro, course presents a detailed look at how various systems work and describes basic IT problem-solving techniques. Familiarization with hardware and software, as well as trends in IT, is also covered. Many of these introductory courses feature group work and hands-on projects that are completed in the classroom and/or computer labs.

Ergonomics are important in IT classes. Look for workstations, monitors, lighting, and seating that help prevent eye and body fatigue during long computer sessions.

In addition to these technology-specific disciplines, basic communication skills are essential in every information technology workplace. Therefore, enrollment in a four-year bachelor's degree IT program will include a number of required and elective classes that prepare students to share non-digital ideas and concepts with classmates and coworkers. Most bachelor's degree programs are structured to prepare students for more than the technical aspects of a career. A college education helps students understand and appreciate the world of

LEARNING THE LANGUAGE

At the introductory level, professors explore these concepts starting with a widely used object-oriented computer language, such as Visual BASIC or Java.

Visual BASIC is a computer programming system developed and owned by Microsoft. It was originally created in 1991 to make it easier to write programs for the Windows operating system used in many personal computers. Visual BASIC evolved from a programming language called BASIC (Beginner's All-Purpose Symbolic Instruction Code) that was invented in 1963 by two Dartmouth College professors and later purchased by Microsoft's cofounders.

Java is a programming language and computing platform first released by Sun Microsystems in 1995. There are many applications and websites that will not work on a computer or digital device unless Java is installed. Cell

A good professor who explains things clearly and answers your questions makes learning any computer language easier.

phones, supercomputers, tablets, and game consoles all run Java-based applications. Java is free to download and widely used, making it useful in an introductory computer science course.

ideas and logical thinking, as well as how these concepts influence other ideas.

Courses in English composition, technical writing, literature, and natural science (such as biology, geology, environmental science, etc.) are often required in the early semesters of four-year technology degree programs. Later on, students have the opportunity to take business, finance, and management courses as well.

IT Programs in Action

At DePaul University in Chicago, for example, the IT curriculum covers database construction and management, as well as computer security. Both career fields are very in demand, thanks to recent cases of data hacking and cyber attacks. Courses include Web Development, Object-Oriented Programming, Data Analysis, and Advanced Application Development.

Some introductory information technology courses ask students to do more than just memorize IT terms and other "general survey of IT" tasks. At Marquette University in Milwaukee, Wisconsin, the intro course asks students to act as consultants on a mini-project.

Students develop and generate process flow diagrams and data models, and they conclude the semester by running a database project with Microsoft Access software.

Who Needs a Bachelor's Degree in IT?

The computer industry is far more complex today than when Bill Gates introduced Microsoft Windows, more

PROTECTING DIGITAL DATA

As hackers increasingly target corporations and retailers, the role of a network or computer security specialist becomes more important. Data theft is a huge problem for any organization. When customers' personal information—credit card numbers, e-mail addresses, etc.—falls into the hands of criminals, customers must cancel credit cards and obtain credit-monitoring services. So network security employees work to create firewalls and anti-virus software that defend the organization's servers, computer systems, and data from malware, viruses, hackers, and other attacks designed to steal confidential information. With each new high-profile security breach—Target, Neiman-Marcus, and TJX stores are recent big-name victims of hackers—the demand for network security experts surges.

than thirty years ago, and changes occur more rapidly. New programming languages quickly replace old ones; different versions of software appear and depart, often at a blistering pace. New devices and modes of technology crop up with great frequency. IT professionals must stay current. Enrolling in a four-year degree program, which is often more comprehensive than an associate's degree program or certification training, is one way to do that.

Bachelor's degree programs in IT also typically have a broader base of auxiliary or complementary courses of study, such as business or math. Understanding how today's businesses decide to invest in new technologies, software, and product development may give students more competitive skills that organizations value. A four-year degree will help students gain an understanding of how companies start up, grow, and market their IT innovations.

Perhaps the biggest argument for a four-year degree in IT is that it has become the minimum qualification that hiring managers look for when considering job candidates for IT positions. Consequently, a four-year degree in information technology

Earning a bachelor's degree will give you the necessary qualifications for a wider range of positions in the field of information technology.

can give students increased marketability and mobility. They'll find more opportunities to do great work, move between major players in the IT industry, and possibly have international impact—and enjoy their careers—by completing a bachelor's degree.

What About a Master's Degree?

A master's degree in information technology is required in research and higher-education careers. These advanced degrees may require two or more years to complete and can be beneficial in pursuing management-level positions in organizations, such as chief information officer.

One option for those looking to add a master's degree to their résumé is signing on for a dual-degree program. These are programs that let students work for a bachelor's degree and a master's simultaneously under a five-year plan.

CHAPTER FIVE

Choosing an IT Degree Program

C hoosing a degree program requires a close look at the specific courses and career paths offered. Choosing a university or college is a matter of finding a good fit between an academic institution and a student's study habits, need for interaction with faculty, financial resources, and willingness to try new approaches.

Degrees in Demand

Many colleges offer several degrees that are in demand in the IT and information systems universe. University degree programs help prepare students for careers as systems analysts, systems administrators, and technical support specialists, more commonly called IT technicians. Degree programs in computer network and systems administration will also help students pursue careers in computer and network security, technical operations management, network engineering, and other related IT and information systems work.

Choosing a degree program, which requires deciding on a specific major, can be a challenge due primarily to the sheer number of offerings available. For example, the California State University system has twenty-three campuses offering four-year degrees. Within this system, nearly fifty academic programs are offered that are directly related, or correlate strongly, to the information technology and information systems industry. California's university system offers a website—www.assist.org—that can help sift through different options.

Students can find many online resources to help select the college or university that offers the best mix of IT and elective courses. But speaking with an advisor at a college is always helpful.

There is some overlap among these degrees, so look carefully at the specific course offerings in each degree to ensure a good fit with your career ambitions. For example, the University of Cincinnati in Ohio offers a bachelor's degree in information technology that covers network and systems administration and database management, as well as software application development and digital media. Within this degree program are two distinct tracks. The networking/systems track focuses on studies that support the operation, integration, administration, and security of computer networks. The university's software applications track teaches students how to develop software solutions for users and organizations, whether they are for desktop, web, or mobile computing platforms.

Size, Reputation, and Offerings

Dozens of four-year colleges and universities—including big-name universities such as Baylor, Harvard, Stanford, and MIT—offer bachelor's degrees in information technology and its related fields. A smaller four-year college would have a smaller IT department but will cover comparable academic content, often with the added benefit of being able to give more personalized attention to individual students. Either way, students receive a rich, varied education in IT and information systems.

Choosing a program can be challenging. Where to start? Factors that students should weigh include class sizes, the college environment, study abroad

WHERE YOU GO, WHO YOU KNOW

There's a popular belief—and a certain amount of anecdotal evidence—that suggests the particular university that awards a degree makes a difference. Some of this has to do with the reputation a particular college or university might have. Another consideration is networking opportunities both before and after graduation.

For example, Facebook CEO Mark Zuckerberg attended Harvard University in Massachusetts and is familiar with IT and computer science graduates of East Coast colleges that may include Massachusetts Institute of Technology, Dartmouth College, and Harvard. Sergey Brin and Larry Page, cofounders of Google, met at Stanford University in California and knew many West Coast computer science stars. In 1999, they hired another Stanford graduate—Marissa Mayer—as only their twentieth employee. She helped develop Google Maps, Gmail, and Google Earth. In 2012, Mayer became the president and CEO of Yahoo, Inc.

programs, extracurricular offerings, and the diversity of students and faculty.

Another consideration is what value a degree from a specific university has out in the workplace. Check out what graduates from different universities have done with their IT-related degrees by reading online alumni stories and career profiles. Many colleges talk about the percentage of graduates hired quickly after graduation, but it is their alumni stories that show how a degree helped them progress in the work world.

More Than Tech

It's important to remember that a four-year degree program should include courses that develop both technical and analytical skills, plus the ability to communicate and think logically. Many IT degree programs also require courses in science, the humanities, and topics that prepare students for life's many opportunities, both creative and professional.

Career fairs provide good opportunities to speak with IT and information systems professionals, as well as asking hiring managers about current and future job openings.

For example, the B.S. degree in information technology at Rochester Institute of Technology in Rochester, New York, requires courses such as Discrete Mathematics, Computer Problem Solving, Foundations of Modern Information Processing, Applied Calculus, Ethics in Computing, Designing the User Experience, and more. The RIT degree also asks you to take courses in liberal arts and sciences, a broad category that includes options in philosophy, political science, sociology and anthropology, psychology, economics, and others. These requirements help you learn how to interact with others in your career.

Looking for a smaller technology college experience? One example is Michigan Technological University (MTU) in Houghton, Michigan. Its bachelor's program in computer network and systems administration (CSNA) prepares students for work in computer and network security, network engineering, VoIP (voice-over Internet protocol, or online telecommunications), Linux systems, and other popular IT roles. Core courses in MTU's major include Computer and Operating Systems Architecture, Network Administration, Computer-Cyber Ethics/Policy, Database Management, Unix and Linux Administration, Mobile Computing and FCC Regulations, Network Security Engineering, Computer Networks and System Administration, and more.

Physical and Virtual Campuses

For some students, the experience of a physical college campus, where students meet with faculty and classmates daily, is a big plus. This type of environment enhances the learning experience. Many students prefer real-time conversations with classmates and scheduled classes and labs. They prefer to meet with a professor in a lab or office after class to get more detailed explanations of complex ideas. These are a few of the benefits —along with living away from home—that are offered by attending a brick-and-mortar college. However, housing and meal costs are often an added expense when attending a physical college campus.

Other students find online or distance learning more appealing, as online classmates may include people from other countries and adult learners. Students interact or chat with their classmates and professors in online discussion forums. Online courses enable students to read or view lectures, complete assignments, and submit quizzes at any time of day or night. Flexible scheduling and exchange of ideas with professors and students anytime make an online degree program an attractive choice. That's why many conventional colleges and universities offer online degree programs or a mix of online and in-class courses.

Here, a student at MassBay Community College works with a computer science professor. MassBay's computer science course was designed in conjunction with Massachusetts Institute of Technology, a four-year university.

The For-Profit Option

In addition, for-profit colleges—those that are run by private-sector organizations and corporations—offer online computer science degrees. Consider an information technology degree offered by Kaplan University, a for-profit online college. Depending on the study track

EXPLORING ONLINE DEGREES

A little exploration can help show whether online study or physical classrooms are right for you. Online or distance courses are popular for their convenience but won't necessarily save tuition money over a brick-and-mortar college. Tuition fees are comparable. An online degree program has no residence or dining halls, however, so your money mostly goes for tuition, not room and board.

Some conventional universities offer prospective students the chance to try an online course. A number of colleges—including big-name universities such as Harvard, Stanford, MIT, and others—offer introductory online courses in information technology. For example, Stanford University offers An Introduction to Computer Networks, a six-week overview that features videos, exercises, and guest lectures. University of California at Berkeley and other universities share video lectures online.

chosen, the program will prepare students to design real-world e-media products, such as online games and apps, or create technical solutions to hardware and software problems. Students learn how to communicate and apply information technologies professionally, as well as evaluate, design, and implement systems based on IT procedures.

The Kaplan IT degree offers two tracks, in applied technology and information systems. The applied technology track focuses on how to use and manage various information systems and technologies to serve the needs of employees, customers, and organizations. Coursework is geared toward a career as a network administrator, who makes sure that an organization's network, servers, and data operate reliably. Courses include Programming Fundamentals for Beginners, Introduction to Website Development, Software Applications, College Algebra, writing classes, and courses to help you act professionally in the workplace, plus electives.

The information systems track deals with creating and managing information systems, databases, and technologies. It also includes an introductory course on information systems architecture, plus coursework in business and communication skills. This track is geared for careers in database management, information security and forensics, and multiplatform software development. Courses in this track differ a bit from the applied technology track and include Foundations in Information Technology, Database Foundations, Network Security, Systems Analysis and Design, Project Management, and related topics and electives.

CHAPTER SIX

Taking a Different Road

I n recent years, more and more students have been studying to earn an IT degree. A 2011 Computing Research Association report indicated that enrollment in all computer-related career programs, including IT, had increased for three years prior to that. Today's IT professionals work in hospitals, corporations, universities, and government. They work hard, solve problems for coworkers and clients, earn good salaries, and have time to enjoy their families and friends outside the workplace.

However, not everyone takes the same path to a career in IT or information systems. As some "old economy" manufacturing jobs went away, people with outdated skills returned to college to take IT courses

Shadowing an IT professional in his or her work environment is a great way to understand the day-to-day responsibilities of today's computing world.

that helped them compete for new jobs. Also, students with degrees in fields as diverse as biology, physics, graphic arts, and mathematics have gone on to success as IT professionals.

The road to a career in IT and information systems doesn't always include earning a degree in IT or information systems. Employers may also consider a student's drive and discipline to complete a four- or five-year degree when deciding who to hire, as well as coursework that corresponds to the responsibilities of the job without the benefit of a strictly IT degree. That's basically what happened for the IT professionals profiled in this chapter.

Crossing Connected Careers

Many IT professionals came to their current roles from finance, health care, science, and business operations. When their employers discovered a need for IT workers, they often enlisted employees who understood the specific information IT users would rely upon. For example, nurses and physicians in hospitals use computer networks and complex software to document how they diagnose and treat patients. IT professionals install, maintain, and troubleshoot both the software and the networks on which medical professionals work. Sometimes nurses, doctors, and other medical professionals with some IT experience work alongside information systems colleagues to make sure systems perform as required.

Some IT professionals believe it's wiser to focus on a broad-based degree, rather than on one area

Few surgeons and nurses start out in IT, but the expectations of today's health care industry require them to document diagnoses and treatment procedures for every patient.

(such as network administration, web development, or IT security). As an example, consider the career path taken by Mary T. Martin, who manages IT applications and data reporting at a Rochester, New York, health imaging technology company. As an undergraduate, Martin studied to earn a bachelor's degree in business administration and accounting, not information technology. In fact, she had to be creative when taking any type of computer class.

"There was just one Intro to Computer Science class at my college at the time," she said. "I went to Rochester Institute of Technology through a reciprocal program to pick up other computer science theory courses, where I learned about BASIC [a programming language]."

Martin went on to earn a graduate degree in computer information systems and finance from the University of Rochester. She now leads a team of business information analysts.

MAKING A LIVING

Careers in IT and information systems generally pay better than physical labor jobs. Organizations often compete for well-educated IT candidates with good salary and benefits packages. Several websites collect and share salary ranges for different IT jobs, including Salary.com, Indeed.com, and GlassDoor.com. But keep in mind that salaries will vary. It costs more to live in large cities in the Northeast (e.g. Boston and New York) or on the West Coast (e.g. Los Angeles and San Francisco), so salaries for the same job in those areas may be different than salaries in smaller towns in the South, West, and Midwestern United States. *The Occupational Outlook Handbook* published by the U.S. Department of Labor is another resource for checking salaries, as well as the outlook for jobs over the coming years.

From Criminal Justice to Quality Assurance

Making sure that new software or applications work among the many devices and locations in an organization is an important IT role. The person who fills this position needs to have experience in the technology and IT fields, although not necessarily an IT degree.

Take, for example, Jason Stinson, who earned a four-year degree in criminal justice. He began his career as a technical writer in the IT industry, rather than the field he studied in college. After learning HTML, style sheets, and JavaScript, he used his tech-writing experience to get an entry-level job at Amazon.com when the company was just getting started.

After that, he took a few other West Coast positions, then relocated to western New York, where he became a software quality assurance and testing manager for a regional hospital system. Today, his job entails helping to ensure that

Medical professionals and hospital staffs share patient information on computers, tablets, and smartphones. Software development in the health care field is in high demand.

upgrades and improvements to a complex electronic medical records system function as designed.

Further Off the Path

Joel Rosen began pursuing an associate's degree but put it aside once he found steady employment. He worked for about fifteen years until discovering that the lack of a formal degree limited his ability to land more senior positions. So he went back to college, first earning the liberal arts credits that would enable him to enter a four-year program at Virginia Commonwealth University, where he earned a bachelor of fine arts degree.

"After graduating, I went immediately to RIT, [and completed an] MFA program in computer graphics, which led to working at Kodak as an interaction designer, primarily focused on the web, but also on other screen-based interactive experiences [kiosks]," he said.

Today, Rosen works as a lead experience architect at Effective UI, a company that creates market-ready digital products, web applications, and mobile apps.

The bottom line is that completing a degree is often necessary to compete for IT jobs and earn the respect of employers and peers. But the degree need not always be in IT to launch a career in information technology.

CHAPTER SEVEN

What Employers Look for in IT

To provide an idea of what employers expect in a candidate for a job in information technology, consider the following job postings for two different IT positions with a regional bank.

Employment Posting No. 1

The first posting is for a programmer analyst to design, install, and support software and programs that help manage the bank's data so that it can better serve its customers. This work includes learning the data-management needs from the bank's product managers, who study the data, and working with those managers to develop clear, detailed software requirements that everyone agrees upon. Then the analyst would work to create, install (or implement), and document the programming that meets the bank's needs within an agreed-upon timeframe.

The programmer analyst is also expected to make sure his or her programming solutions are reliable. When changes are necessary, the employee must schedule those changes and perform any upgrades so that they don't disrupt the bank's regular operations (often making these changes at night or on weekends). His or her IT manager would expect the programmer analyst to be available ("on call") to support the programming solution when it's in use.

Notice the background the employer is looking for, particularly with regard to degree requirements and skills/working knowledge:

Many jobs in information technology require employees to do work after regular office hours. This may mean working from home or staying late at the office.

- Bachelor of science in computer science or equivalent degree
- Programming skills utilizing SQL (short for Structured Query Language)
- Experience with .NET, including Visual BASIC and C#
- Documentation, analysis (including requirements gathering and estimation), and design skills
- Effective communications, interpersonal, and team-building skills

- Proven ability to manage activities with limited guidance
- Knowledge of web and client server solutions

The advertisement states clearly that a four-year bachelor's degree is required, although it does not specify that the degree be one in IT or information systems. That automatically seems to mean that people with IT certification need not apply. However, the bank also would like to hire someone with hands-on experience in

Replacing a computer's power supply or motherboard sounds complicated, but the right training in computer hardware makes these tasks as easy as changing a lightbulb.

DEGREE-BOOSTING INTERNSHIPS

When deciding what degree they should work toward obtaining to enter the information technology and information systems fields, prospective technicians may want to factor in whether or not a school's IT programs offer on-the-job training while the student is still in school. Internships are available at virtually every school, particularly those with four-year degree programs. Because hands-on experience in the workplace looks great on a résumé, internships are invaluable.

Speaking of value, some internships are paid positions. If they do get paid (many don't), interns receive what's called a stipend, a small sum of money they get throughout their time at work. As an intern, a college student might get some kind of certificate when his or her training is completed. More likely, the intern's supervisor will write a letter of recommendation, which tells future employers that the student is a good worker and has at least basic knowledge of the job tasks of the field. In some cases, interns who perform very well are asked to stay on at a company or organization and are made permanent, paid employees.

a number of IT-related areas. Certification coursework at a vocational school emphasizes the more practical aspects of a career field. This means that students in these programs perform many tasks in addition to learning about them from a teacher or reading about them in a book. So while certification alone would not win an applicant the programmer analyst job, someone who had a bachelor's degree and certification could actually have a leg up on the competition.

Example Job Posting No. 2

A senior business systems analyst at this bank is a role with more planning, analysis, and troubleshooting duties. The senior analyst often works with other IT professionals, and a few of the expectations are similar to those of the programmer analyst. For this particular position, the senior analyst is expected to manage projects with different users' needs in mind. He or she must have a broader background in analyzing a business's information technology needs. The senior analyst needs to understand how creating and installing the software will help improve the bank's productivity over time.

As posted in the advertisement, the job's requirements are:

- Bachelor's degree in a technical field or related experience that demonstrates use of advanced analytical skills
- Minimum of five years' experience in supporting the business aspects of application systems

- Adept in all aspects of the software development life cycle, including gathering requirements, design, implementation, testing, and support
- Competency in relational database concepts and SQL
- Understanding of banking products, services, and supporting business processes and technologies
- Demonstrated knowledge of application configuration and packaged software integration
- Very good analysis and design skills
- Effective organization, communications, interpersonal, and team-building skills
- Proven ability to multitask and independently manage complex activities
- Proven ability to follow a predetermined set of standards and process flow

Note that for this senior analyst job, the requirements don't specifically ask for an IT or computer science degree. The bank wants a background in technology, but degrees in mathematics, business, finance, software development, or network administration and security may also be considered. The business systems analyst in this job is expected to understand the bank's overall business functions—not just its information systems—and how his or her software solutions help those functions run more effectively.

The bottom line is that this bank needs IT people in each of the positions who can understand how the work they do helps make the bank more productive, efficient, secure, and profitable. If the knowledge a student gains in his or her degree studies helps solve these problems, he or she will be an attractive candidate.

Summing Up

When considering career choices in information technology and information systems, start by looking at job listings online and understanding the skills and training employers ask for. Job posting sites such as Indeed.com, Monster, Simply Hired, and others allow students to look at different positions and their requirements.

Remember, more than a few of today's IT professionals started their careers in different pursuits and later entered the IT field with business experience that helped them grow into their IT roles. They earned four-year degrees that helped them get hired, then navigated toward jobs that drew upon their business experience to improve IT functions in the organization. The upshot is that many roads can lead future IT professionals to their ultimate career destination.

The "anytime, anywhere" Wi-Fi networks of college campuses enable students to work on assignments and projects whenever they find free time.

CHAPTER EIGHT

Learning After College: Class Is Never Dismissed

I n most professions, advances in technology take place every few years. Electronics and automation replace mechanical and manual processes. Doctors need to be recertified as new treatments and diagnosis techniques are found. IT workers often need to refresh their skills in information technology as well. In fact, in the information technology field, upgrading one's skills is a way of life. Hardware changes often, as more network functions take place on laptops and handheld tablets. Sometimes industry-wide standards change, such as when Microsoft rolls out a new version of Windows that renders older versions obsolete. Web pages that once relied on HTML or XML are moving to a more sophisticated platform, HTML5. Whether IT professionals are responsible for network security, developing software for apps, or managing complex databases, they can expect to need to refresh their knowledge every three to five years.

To help keep their skills current, IT workers must plan to devote a portion of their time to learning, even after college. After a few years at a job, employees

To keep abreast of new developments in IT, even experienced systems professionals often attend training programs that provide new certifications and insights.

usually get a sense of the particular duties that interest them the most. Those duties may be expanded, and offer better pay, under a different job title. Continuing education can help employees learn new skills required for other IT positions, in addition to being the smart path to upgrading current skills.

Make a Plan

Some businesses ask their employees to create a professional development plan to help spell out anticipated growth opportunities. This is a written plan outlining a person's job goals, as well as thought-out, step-by-step ways to achieve those goals. Companies use these plans as a way to help workers stay well trained, but also as a yardstick to help managers judge how well an employee meets his or her pre-set goals. The plans sometimes become part of an employee's performance appraisal, which is used to determine whether a pay raise or promotion is in order.

So who really benefits from having a plan in place, the employee or the company? An employee gets the most out of a professional development plan if he or she uses it to identify professional strengths and gaps and if it spells out what training he or she needs to remain productive.

The same is true for an employee's long-term goals. Working as a programmer analyst or IT technician is fine for a first or second IT job. As an employee gains experience, however, he or she might want to take on more responsibilities, lead teams, and coach and mentor new hires—and be compensated for those added roles. A personal development plan helps map out the steps he or she needs to grow professionally and identify training options that will help strengthen his or her skills.

Taking ownership of a development plan is essential. The plan doesn't belong to the boss and should not be tied to the success of a single company. Remember, businesses can be sold, merged, or closed, so a professional development plan should consider these scenarios. What skills would a database administrator need if the company were sold to a larger organization, such as Oracle or Microsoft?

Today's marketplace requires most professionals to map out their career plans and think about other industries in which their skills might be in demand.

Understanding where certain IT skills are most in demand is also important. For example, a security analyst for a maker of health document management applications and systems knows there are a few big companies in this category, plus smaller ones, so takeovers are a possibility. If this analyst enjoys working in health care, he or she should think about other businesses that need those analytic IT skills, such as hospitals, home care agencies, health insurance companies, and medical practices.

Write a plan, but don't hide it in a desk drawer. Pull it out and review it at least twice a year. An employee's interests can change—say, from website design to network security systems—so it's a good idea to update a plan to focus on training that will make it easier to choose a new career direction.

Continuing Learning Options for IT Professionals

Many companies have learned that it's more expensive to hire and train new staff than to keep a current

employee and invest in new training. So these companies set aside a portion of their budget for employee
training. As a rule of thumb, larger companies are more
likely to provide such training, while smaller businesses
offer fewer external training opportunities; they sometimes choose online training providers to help refresh
employees' skills.

Industry-leading tech companies—think Microsoft,
Oracle, and Google—may sponsor in-house professional
development or academies designed to help employers
strengthen their employees' skills. Employers sometimes pay for continued classroom training or work
toward another degree program, such as a master's,
as well. Participants must earn more than a passing
grade, however, for the employer to reimburse the cost
of the course. Anyone choosing to take advantage of
employer-supported training should keep in mind that
any training will take time and that pursuing a master's
degree while working a full-time job will take longer than
a couple of semesters, whether it's done online or in a
classroom.

There are other postgraduate training options that
can be pursued, often through a professional organization or a large manufacturer of software or applications.
Local professional organizations offer webinars, manufacturer's demonstrations, online learning, and guest
lectures; these are a good way to pick up current
insights. If certification is needed on a specific software
or application, search online to see if the manufacturer
or a university offers any e-learning opportunities.

Some community colleges and universities
offer training opportunities that small and mid-size

MICROSOFT CERTIFICATION

As one of the world's largest software and application developers, Microsoft provides training and certifications—including exams—to help IT employees gain and demonstrate mastery of Microsoft products. Certification programs are offered in servers (such as Windows, Lync, and Exchange), desktop systems, database (SQL), applications (such as Office, Office 365, and Microsoft Dynamics), and developer applications (such as Visual Studio, Windows Phone, and SharePoint). Learn more at http://www.microsoft.com/learning/en-us/default.aspx.

businesses can find beneficial. In communities that have seen jobs shift from manufacturing to information technology, some area colleges have created economic development programs designed to help employers refresh the skills of their workforce. For example, Monroe Community College in Rochester, New York, offers training opportunities tailored to the needs of computer operators and IT professionals. In addition to the Microsoft certifications described in the sidebar, others include certifications in Cisco networking, Oracle database administration, Java updates, software testing, and PC/Network technician functions.

Safe and Secure

No matter what job an IT worker has, he or she must always be aware of computer security issues. Threats from hackers and cyberattacks are a big concern for every organization. Looking into post-degree coursework in cybersecurity would be wise no matter what IT degree a person holds. Two popular certificates in this area are the Certified Ethical Hacker (CEH) and the Certified Information Security System Professional (CISSP).

CISSP certification reflects today's high concern with network security, protecting personal and corporate data, and the threat of hacking. This certificate recognizes mastery of an international standard for information security, and the certification is managed by the International Information Systems Security Certification Consortium (ISC2). Certification can enhance a professional's career and provide added credibility when pursuing career opportunities. To earn the certificate, an employee must already have five years' worth of IT experience, which can be waived if a person passes a test based on his or her experience in other information security areas certified by ISC2. These include cryptography, access control, and software development security, among others. The learning process includes an exam, webcasts, in-classroom training via seminars, and real-time or self-paced online learning.

The CEH certificate program helps an employee learn to test, hack, and secure systems in the workplace. Participants also learn about intrusion detection, policy creation, social engineering, DDoS (distributed denial of

Threats from hackers and cyberattacks have created a demand for Certified Ethical Hackers and other computer security experts who can combat online attacks and Internet censorship.

service) attacks, buffer overflows, and virus creation. To become a Certified Ethical Hacker, students can select from several options offered by the International Council of E-Commerce Consultants (EC-Council.org). Study options include live, online, instructor-led classes; an on-site training paid for by an employer or other parent organization; self-paced "iLearn" training modules; or downloading the courseware for self-study. Each option has fees and costs.

Earning either of these certificates could be a smart move on the part of an employee. Holding them tells current or potential employers that the employee understands how to deal with malicious threats to IT operations.

Putting It All Together

Earning a degree in information technology makes any graduate an attractive candidate for a job in the IT field. But earning a degree—whether it's an associate's, bachelor's, master's, or even a doctorate—isn't the end of a student's professional growth. The technologies, software, and languages of IT and information systems change and evolve with surprising frequency. To keep up with these relentless changes, experienced IT employees need more training within a few years after earning their degrees.

It's the employee's responsibility to plan for career changes and professional growth and take advantage of learning opportunities within and outside the workplace. Keeping up with industry changes is the best way to remain competitive in the IT employment marketplace and become attractive to potential new employers later on.

With society's ever-growing reliance on IT and information systems to conduct everyday business and social interactions, career opportunities in this field are only expected to grow. The many degree options offered both online and in conventional college classrooms can put students with hopes of becoming a valued systems administrator, systems analyst, IT technician, or the like on the right track.

GLOSSARY

academic Having to do with schools, education, and learning.

algorithm A set of mathematical instructions designed to make a computer perform a specific task.

alumni People who attended and graduated from a certain high school, college, or university.

application A self-contained computer program that operates without using a built-in browser; known as "app" for short.

associate's degree A two-year degree program concentrating on a major and other basic courses.

bachelor's degree A four- or five-year degree program emphasizing a major course of study, plus electives.

certification Official acknowledgement of having completed training or a course of study.

database administrator An IT worker responsible for the performance, integrity, and security of a database.

doctorate The highest degree a student can earn in a particular field of study.

firewall Software program or hardware that helps screen out hackers and computer viruses.

firmware Software that is programmed into the fixed or permanent memory of an electronic device.

malware Software that can slow, corrupt, or damage a computer system; an abbreviated term for "malicious software."

master's degree A postgraduate program involving in-depth analysis of an academic discipline.

programmer analyst Person who analyzes information systems and writes applications for a system.

quality assurance analyst Person responsible for maintaining software quality within an organization.

SQL Structured Query Language, used to create, transform, and retrieve information (pronounced "sequel").

systems administrator Person who manages the computer systems (especially hardware) in an organization.

systems analyst Employee who designs, develops, and modifies an information system based on user requirements.

technical support specialist Employee who provides assistance to solve software or hardware problems.

FOR MORE INFORMATION

Association for Computing Machinery (ACM)
2 Penn Plaza, Suite 701
New York, NY 10121-0701
(800) 342-6626
Website: http://www.acm.org
ACM focuses on professional development and promot-
ing policies and research that benefit society. It hosts
a digital library and serves global members with
journals and magazines, conferences, workshops,
electronic forums, and an online learning center.

Association of Information Technology Professionals
(AITP)
15000 Commerce Parkway, Suite C
Mount Laurel, NJ 08054
(800) 224-9371
Website: http://www.aitp.org
Founded in 1951, AITP works to advance the IT field
through professional development, support of IT
education, and national policies on IT that seek to
improve society as a whole.

Canadian Health Information Management Association
(CHIMA)
99 Enterprise Drive, South, Lower Level
London, ON N6N 1B9
Canada
(877) 332-4462
Website: http://www.echima.ca
CHIMA represents about 5,000 Health Information
Management professionals, offering certification

programs and supporting continuing education and professional practice of HIM professionals.

Canadian Information Processing Society (CIPS)
5090 Explorer Drive, Suite 801
Mississauga, ON L4W 4T9
Canada
(877) ASK-CIPS (275-2477)
Website: http://www.cips.ca
CIPS is an association of individual IT professionals that helps establish standards and share best practices. The organization offers networking opportunities, certification of IT professionals, an IT job board, and accreditation of postsecondary training programs.

Institute of Electrical and Electronics Engineers (IEEE)
3 Park Avenue, 17th Floor
New York, NY 10016
(212) 419-7900
Website: http://www.ieee.org
IEEE is the world's largest technical professional association, serving professionals who use information technology, including software developers, information technology professionals, and computer scientists.

ISACA
3701 Algonquin Road, Suite 1010
Rolling Meadows, IL 60008
(847) 253-1545
Website: http://www.isaca.org
ISACA serves about 110,000 members worldwide who are interested or employed in IT audit,

information security risk, and IT governance
fields.

Women in Technology (WIT)
10378 Democracy Lane, Suite A
Fairfax, VA 22030
(703) 766-1153
Website: http://www.womenintechnology.org
Women in Technology is a professional organization
focused on the professional development of women
in computing, engineering, and related fields.

Women in Technology International Professional
Association (WITI)
Olympic Plaza
11500 Olympic Boulevard, Suite 400
Los Angeles, CA 90064
(818) 788-9484
Website: http://www.witi.com
This global organization is focused on improving
workplace opportunities for women in information
technology and information systems management.

Websites

Because of the changing nature of Internet links,
Rosen Publishing has developed an online list of
websites related to the subject of this book. This
site is updated regularly. Please use the following
link to access the list:

http://www.rosenlinks.com/RDFM/Info

FOR FURTHER READING

Alpern, Naomi J., Joey Alpern, and Randy Muller. *IT Career Jumpstart: An Introduction to PC Hardware, Software, and Networking.* Indianapolis, IN: John Wiley & Sons, 2012.

Bolles, Richard N. *What Color Is Your Parachute? 2014: A Practical Manual for Job-Hunters and Career-Changers.* Berkeley, CA: Ten-Speed Press, 2013.

College Board. *Book of College Majors, All-New 51st Edition.* New York, NY: The College Board/MacMillan, 2013.

Ferguson Publishing. *Careers in Focus: Technicians.* New York, NY: Ferguson Publishing, 2010.

Fiske, Edward. *The Fiske Guide to Colleges 2014.* Naperville, IL: Sourcebooks, 2013.

Freedman, Jeri. *Careers in Computer Support* (Careers in Computer Technology). New York, NY: Rosen Publishing, 2013.

Grayson, Robert. *Careers in Network Engineering* (Careers in Computer Technology). New York, NY: Rosen Publishing, 2011.

Harmon, Daniel E. *Careers in Internet Security* (Careers in Computer Technology). New York, NY: Rosen Publishing, 2011.

Indovino, Shaina. *Women in Information Technology.* Broomall, PA: Mason Crest Publishers, 2013.

McCormick, Lisa. *Financial Aid Smarts: Getting Money for School* (Get Smart with Your Money). New York, NY: Rosen Publishing, 2012.

Meyer, Terry Teague. *The Vo-Tech Track to Success in Information Technology* (Learning a Trade,

Preparing for a Career). New York, NY: Rosen Publishing, 2014.

Meyers, Michael. *Comp TIA A+ Certification All-in-One Exam Guide.* Columbus, OH: McGraw-Hill, 2012.

Reeves, Diane Lindsey. *Career Ideas for Teens in Information Technology.* New York, NY: Ferguson Publishing, 2012.

Ryan, Robin. *60 Seconds and You're Hired.* New York, NY: Penguin Books, 2008.

Silivanch, Annalise. *Making the Right College Choice (Thinking About College).* New York, NY: Rosen Publishing, 2010.

Vogelstein, Fred. *Dogfight: How Apple and Google Went to War and Started a Revolution.* New York, NY: Sarah Crichton Books, 2013.

Wilson, Patrick. *Health IT JumpStart: The Best First Step Toward an IT Career in Health Information Technology.* Hoboken, NJ: Sybex Publishing, 2011.

BIBLIOGRAPHY

Baylor University. "Undergraduate Costs at a Glance." Retrieved January 9, 2014 (http://www.baylor.edu/ admissions/index.php?id=82223).

Biography.com. "Marissa Mayer biography." Retrieved January 9, 2014 (http://www.biography.com/ people/marissa-mayer-20902689).

Coppinger, James. "CAD Designers: What Do They Actually Do?" About.com. Retrieved January 7, 2014 (http://cad.about.com/od/CAD_Jobs/a/Cad -Designers.htm and http://cad.about.com/od/CAD_ Jobs/a/What-Is-A-Cad-Manager.htm).

DePaul University Staff. "Information Technology." DePaul University. Retrieved February 12, 2014 (http://www .depaul.edu/academics/undergraduate/majors/ Pages/itbs.aspx).

ESL Federal Credit Union. "Career Opportunities." Retrieved January 10, 2014 (http://www.esl.org).

Humboldt State University. "Five-Year Course Plan in Computer Science." April 10, 2013. Retrieved January 7, 2014 (http://www.humboldt.edu/ computerscience/docs/CS%20FiveYrPlan%20 2012-2017.pdf).

Hunter College. "Computer Technician Certificate." Retrieved February 12, 2014 (http://www.hunter.cuny .edu/ce/certificates/computer/computer-technician -certificate).

Kaplan University. "Bachelor of Science in Information Technology Degree." Retrieved January 15, 2014 (http://www.kaplanuniversity.edu/information -technology/information-technology-bachelor -degree-info-systems.aspx).

League of Professional Systems Administrators. "Colleges with System Admin Degrees." September 7, 2012. Retrieved February 12, 2014 (https://lopsa .org/content/colleges-system-admin-degrees).

Lee, Brian. "Network Security Specialist." Retrieved January 8, 2014 (http://computer-careers-review .toptenreviews.com/network-security-specialis t-review.html).

Lytle, Ryan. "Computer Science Continues Growth on College Campuses." *U.S. News & World Report,* July 12, 2012. Retrieved January 15, 2014 (http://www.usnews.com/education/best-colleges/ articles/2012/07/12/computer-science-continues -growth-on-college-campuses).

Mabbutt, Dan. "What Is Visual BASIC?" About.com. Retrieved January 7, 2014 (http://visualbasic .about.com/od/applications/a/whatisvb.htm).

Marquette University. "Introduction to Information Technology." Retrieved February 12, 2014 (http:// www.mu.edu/~owt/mana120.html).

Michielsen, Erik. "How to Choose a College Major You Can Use All Your Life." August 29, 2012. Retrieved January 7, 2014 (http://youtu.be/ yOIc845yAws).

Michigan Technological University. "Computer Network and System Administration." Retrieved February 13, 2014 (http://www.mtu.edu/ technology/undergraduate/cnsa).

Microsoft Corporation. "Learning." Retrieved January 7, 2014 (http://www.microsoft.com/learning/ en-us/default.aspx).

Monroe Community College. "Academic Programs."
    Retrieved January 8, 2014 (http://www.monroecc
    .edu/etsdbs/MCCatPub.nsf/AcademicPrograms
    ?OpenPage).
Monroe Community College. "Economic Development
    and Workforce Services." Retrieved January 8,
    2014 (http://www.monroecc.edu/workforce).
Northern Virginia Community College. "NOVA Catalog—
    Program of Study." Retrieved February 12, 2014
    (http://www.nvcc.edu/catalog/cat2013/academics/
    programs).
Oracle Academy. "Advanced Computer Science."
    Retrieved January 7, 2014 (https://academy.oracle
    .com/oa-web-advancedcs-description.html).
Oracle Corporation. "What Is Java and Why Do I need
    It?" Retrieved January 10, 2014 (http://www.java
    .com/en/download/faq/whatis_java.xml).
Prolexic Knowledge Center. "What Is a DDoS Denial of
    Service?" Prolexic Technologies. Retrieved January
    14, 2014 (http://www.prolexic.com/knowledge
    -center-what-is-ddos-denial-of-service.html?gclid
    =CKHQ1e6WnLwCFZPm7AodSUwAow).
Randall, Eric. "Bill Gates Says He Didn't Have to Drop
    Out of Harvard to Start Microsoft." Boston Maga-
    zine, September 27, 2013. Retrieved January 15,
    2014 (http://www.bostonmagazine.com/news/
    blog/2013/09/27/bill-gates-says-didnt-drop
    -harvard-start-microsoft).
Rochester Institute of Technology. "Welcome to Inter-
    active Games and Media." Retrieved January 15,
    2014 (http://games.rit.edu).

Schurr, Arthur. "Women of Color in IT: Few Confident, Learning and Leading." Diversity/Careers in Engineering and IT. Retrieved February 10, 2014 (http://diversitycareers.com/articles/pro/13-decjan/fod_women.htm).

Scivicque, Chrissy. "Creating Your Professional Development Plan: 3 Surprising Truths." Forbes.com, June 21, 2011. Retrieved January 15, 2014 (http://www.forbes.com/sites/work-in-progress/2011/06/21/creating-your-professional-development-plan-3-surprising-truths).

Taylor, Marissa. "A Career in Information Technology." *Wall Street Journal,* September 13, 2010. Retrieved January 20, 2014 (http://online.wsj.com/news/articles/SB10001424052748704358904575478133397664058).

Texas Southmost College. "Advantages of Attending a Community College." October 23, 2013. Retrieved January 6, 2014 (http://www.tsc.edu/index.php/new-students/advantages-of-attending-a-community-college.html).

University of Cincinnati. "Information Technology." Retrieved February 12, 2014 (https://webapps.uc.edu/DegreePrograms/Program.aspx?ProgramQuickFactsID=1207&ProgramOutlineID=97).

University of Washington. "Choosing a Certificate Program." Retrieved January 6, 2014 (http://www.pce.uw.edu/resources/advising/choosing-certificate.html).

U.S. Department of Labor. *Occupational Outlook Handbook—2013–2014.* St. Paul, MN: JIST Works, 2013.

U.S. News & World Report. "Texas Tech University: Paying for College." Retrieved January 9, 2014 (http://colleges.usnews.rankingsandreviews.com/best-colleges/texas-tech-university-3644/paying?int=c6b9e3).

U.S. News & World Report. "Top Online Bachelor Degree Programs, University Directory." Retrieved January 7, 2014 (http://www.usnewsuniversitydirectory.com/bachelors/technology.aspx).

Victor Valley College. "Guidance and Counseling Center—Degrees and Certificates, How They Work!" January 3, 2014. Retrieved January 9, 2014. (http://www.vvc.edu/offices/guidance_and_counseling/academic.shtml).

White, Martha C. "The $7,000 Computer Science degree—and the Future of Higher Education." *Time*, May 21, 2013. Retrieved January 15, 2014 (http://business.time.com/2013/05/21/the-7000-computer-science-degree-and-the-future-of-higher-education).

INDEX

A

associate's degree program, 16, 17, 20–24, 27, 65
   advantages of, 24–25
   cost considerations, 25–26

B

bachelor's degree, 16, 21, 22, 23, 27, 28, 29, 32–34, 37, 40, 52, 54, 65
Brin, Sergey, 38

C

California State University system, 36
certificate programs, 14, 15–19, 62
Certified Ethical Hacker (CEH), 63–65
Certified Information Security System Professional (CISSP), 63–65
chief information officer, 8
Cincinnati, University of, 37
code/coding, 7–8, 20
community colleges, 13, 21, 22, 24–26, 61
computer network architects, 12
computer support specialists, 6, 12

computer technician certificate, 19
continuing learning, 60–62

D

database administratrors, 6, 8, 10–11
DePaul University (IL), 31
distance/online learning, 18, 21, 28, 41, 42

E

electronics technology certificate, 18–19

F

for-profit colleges, 42–43
four-year degree programs, 13, 19, 21, 22, 23, 24, 26, 27, 28, 36, 37, 39
   bachelor's degree, 16, 21, 22, 23, 27, 28, 29, 32–34, 37, 40, 52, 54, 65
   coursework, 28–31

I

information and network security analysts/specialists, 8, 11, 12, 32
information technology, jobs in, 4–6, 8–12
   outlooks/future of, 11

About the Author

David Kassnoff is a communications professional, writer, and educator with more than twenty years' experience working with information technology professionals and executives in corporate and not-for-profit organizations. His writing has appeared in many mainstream and industry publications, including *American Biotechnology Laboratory*, *Diversity Executive, Profiles in Diversity Journal*, *USA Weekend*, *Audio-Visual Communications*, the Gannett Rochester Newspapers, *Photo Marketing*, *Rochester Business* magazine, the *Los Angeles Times Magazine, Photo Trade News*, and *Practical Homeowner*. He also serves as an adjunct professor in the Russell J. Jandoli School of Journalism and Mass Communication at St. Bonaventure University. His work has been recognized for excellence by the New York State Newspaper Publishers Association and the Council for Advancement and Support of Education.

Photo Credits